# Srinivasa Ramanujan

Sumitha Menon

Srinivasa Ramanujan
*New Horizon Media* ©

First Edition: April 2008
64 Pages
Printed in India.


ISBN 978-81-8368-758-4
Pro-ya-en-14


Prodigy Books
177/103, First Floor,
Ambal's Building, Lloyds Road,
Royapettah, Chennai 600 014.
Ph: +91-44-4200-9603

Email : support@nhm.in
Website : www.nhm.in


Prodigy Books is an imprint of New Horizon Media Private Limited

# Early Days

The story of Srinivasa Ramanujan, the Indian mathematical genius, is both a fairy tale and a tragedy. It is a fairy tale, because it tells the story of a poor Tamil youngster who failed to obtain a degree, becoming elected a Fellow of Trinity College, Cambridge. It is a tragedy because he died at the age of 32, a victim of tuberculosis.

Srinivasa Ramanujan Iyengar was born on 22 December 1887, in Erode, about 400 km from Chennai. He lived with his parents Srinivasa Iyengar and Komalathammal in Sarangapani Street on Kumbakonam, a temple town in Tamil Nadu. When he was two years old, he and his mother shifted to Kanchipuram, another temple town where his mother's parents lived. He had two brothers, Lakshmi Narasimhan, born when Ramanujan was ten and Tirunarayanan, born when he was seventeen. His mother had given birth to a girl and two boys in between. They, however, died in their infancy. So Ramanujan was brought up as an only child, with much love and attention.

The family later returned to Kumbakonam. The city had once been the capital of the ancient Chola empire. Its many temples dating back to that period made Kumbakonam a place of pilgrimage. It was a major town, the sixth largest in the Madras Presidency. Surrounding the town and the districts lay some of the richest cropland in all of India. Rice grew here in abundance, watered generously by the river Kaveri, and the landscape was thick with greenery.

When Ramanujan was growing up, Kumbakonam had a higher proportion of professionals than anywhere else in the Presidency, except Madras. The town also excelled in fine metal work, with its craftsmen creating wonders in copper, silver and brass. The place was also famous for its silk saris, dazzling in bright colours, with eye-catching motifs in silver and gold. Saris woven in Kumbakonam cost as much as Rs 100—a year's earnings for many poor families those days.

Srinivasa Iyengar was a clerk in a sari shop, earning about Rs 20 per month. Ramanujan's mother sang bhajans at a nearby temple, earning five to ten rupees more every month for the family.

At the age of two, Ramanujan suffered from small pox, and carried pock marks for life. But at a time when small pox claimed thousands of lives, Ramanujan was lucky to survive.

As a child, Ramanujan was sensitive, stubborn and self-willed. He sometimes behaved strangely. For example, he sometimes lined up all the brass and copper vessels in the house from one wall to the other. When angry, he would roll in the mud in frustration. He scarcely spoke for the first three years of his life. His worried mother consulted her father's friend. Following his advice, Ramanujan began the practice of 'aksharabhyasam'–his hand, held and guided by his grandfather, was made to draw Tamil characters in a thick bed of rice and each character was spoken aloud. Soon he began to learn the letters of the Tamil alphabet and speak fluently. He was admitted in the local 'pial' school. A 'pial' school was just a teacher and a few pupils in the front porch of a house. Ramanujan did not like school; he felt school curtailed his freedom.

Even as a child, he was very self-directed. Unless he wanted to do something on his own, of his own free will, he did not do it at all. Always quiet and thoughtful, he was forever asking questions. 'Who was the first man in the world?' he wanted to know. 'How far is it between the clouds?' He had no interest in sports and his parents too discouraged him from going out to play. So he was mostly by himself, occasionally talking to friends from the window that overlooked the street. Without exercise, he put on weight, and became quite fat.

Ramanujan was enrolled at Kangeyam Primary School. But when his paternal grandfather died, he had to shift to Madras where his maternal grandparents now lived. He refused to attend school there. His family had to take the help of a local policeman to scare him back to school! After six months at Madras, Ramanujan returned to Kumbakonam.

At Kumbakonam, he was again enrolled in the Kangeyam Primary School. Ramanujan's father hardly spent time with his son. He worked long hours at the shop. His mother was the key figure in his young life. She influenced his ideas, views and outlook. The two spent most of their time together, enjoying each other's intelligent company.

They spent many happy hours playing 'Goats and Tigers', a game played with pebbles and calling for logic, strategy and chess-like concentration. Both mother and son revelled in it.

His mother was a shrewd lady. Her family tree boasted of Sanskrit scholars to whom local kings had bequeathed gifts. She was the daughter of Narayana Iyengar, a court official whose job it was to call witnesses, take down court notes and confer with lawyers. When Ramanujan was four years old, Narayana Iyengar displeased his bosses and lost his job. He then moved to Kanchipuram, a temple city near Madras. There he had the job of managing a choultry attached to a temple where marriages were held and pilgrims stayed.

Ramanujan resembled his mother, Komalathammal. Her powerful personality had a great impact on Ramanujan's life. The two of them were very close. Everyday she fed him curd and rice, sambar and other south Indian delicacies. She combed his hair, tying it in a tuft at the back of his head. She helped him wear his dhoti and applied the 'namam'–caste mark–on his forehead. She walked with him to school. She watched his friends and made decisions for him. She was very religious, held prayer meetings at home and sang devotional songs at the temple. From his mother, Ramanujan learnt all the traditions and principles of his caste and learnt the puranas. He sang religious songs, attended pujas, ate the right food and followed all the rules.

Ramanujan's house stood in Sarangapani Sannidhi Street, a muddy road about thirty feet wide. It was a one-story house thatched with palm leaves, with a covered 'pial' in front. Close to his house was the huge Sarangapani temple, adorned with beautiful sculptures. Ramanujan found the stories of the *Ramayana* and the *Mahabharata* come alive in these images. He came to the temple with his family very often, sometimes during festivals or auspicious days or on other days just to pass the time. He grew up virtually in the shadow of the temple. He eagerly listened to stories about the gods or lectures on the *Bhagavad Gita*.

When Ramanujan was five years old, his family performed the 'upanayanam' ceremony for him. It lasted four days and he was invested with the sacred thread. While growing up, he lived the life of a traditional Brahmin. He wore the 'kutumi,' a tuft at the back of his head, his forehead was shaved and he was strictly vegetarian. He regularly prayed to his family deity, the goddess Namagiri of

Namakkal. He based all his actions on what he thought she wished him to do. He was well versed in the *Vedas*, *Upanishads* and other Hindu scriptures. He attributed to the gods his ability to grasp mathematical texts written in foreign languages. He could recite passages from the *Vedas*, *Sastras* and Sanskrit scriptures and explain their meanings with ease.

The only language Ramanujan's parents knew was Tamil. Many of his friends were from better-off families. They wanted to become lawyers, engineers and government officials. So English was of prime importance to them. Ramanujan also studied English from an early age and in 1897, while a pupil at Kangeyam Primary School, he passed his primary examinations in English, Tamil, arithmetic and geography. He scored the highest marks in the district. The following January, he joined the Town High School.

The school was about a five-minute walk from Ramanujan's house. The best of Kumbakonam's youngsters studied there. For six years, Ramanujan enjoyed his studies there. Here people began to notice his special gifts. His classmates were always rushing to him with mathematical problems. While in the eighth standard, he was challenging his teachers. One day, the mathematics teacher pointed out that anything divided by itself was one. 'Divide three fruits among three people, each will get one. Divide a thousand fruits among a thousand people, each will get one,' said the teacher. Ramanujan immediately asked, 'But is zero divided by zero also one? If no fruits are divided among no one, will each still get one?'

Ramanujan's family, always short of cash, took in boarders for extra income. When he was eleven years old, two boys studying at the nearby government college came to stay with them as paying guests. Seeing Ramanujan's interest in mathematics, they shared whatever they knew with him. Within months, he had exhausted their knowledge and was pestering them for more books from the college library. One of these was an 1893 English textbook on advanced trigonometry by S L Loney. By the time he was thirteen, he had mastered it. He learnt from an older boy how to solve cubic equations. His seniors gave him problems that they thought were difficult. He amazed them by solving them instantly. His teachers and other students were in awe of him. He finished his examinations in half the allotted time and won several merit certificates and scholastic prizes. At a prize-giving function, his headmaster introduced him to the audience as a student who deserved more than 100 marks. Ramanujan had become famous.

# Mathematics Is Not Enough!

While still at school, Ramanujan came across a book, *A Synopsis of Elementary Results in Pure and Applied Mathematics* by George Shoobridge Carr. It had about 5,000 equations in algebra, calculus, trigonometry and analytical geometry with abridged demonstrations of the propositions. This book had a great influence on Ramanujan's career. Fired by enthusiasm, Ramanujan, decided to solve all the problems in Carr's book. In the process of proving one formula, he discovered many others and began to compile his original work in a notebook. Between 1903 and 1914, he filled three notebooks.

After finishing high school, Ramanujan joined Kumbakonam's government college on a scholarship. Totally immersed in mathematics, he lost interest in everything else. At a lecture of history or physiology, his mind wandered. He was always constructing magical tic-tac-toe grids in his mind's eye. These were stuffed with numbers that in every direction would add up to the same quantity. Algebra, trigonometry and calculus ruled his mind. He ignored physiology, English, Greek and roman history. He failed in English Composition and his scholarship was taken away from him. For Ramanujan, the scholarship was a necessity, as his parents were poor. Torn between his passion for mathematics and the compulsion to follow the curriculum, Ramanujan felt miserable. Unable to bear the situation, he ran away from home in August 1905, when he was seventeen years old.

His destination was Visakhapatnam, more than 500 miles from Kumbakonam. No one knows the exact reason why he took off like that. Was he influenced by a friend or did he go seeking a scholarship, patron or a job? His family, worried sick, advertised in the newspapers. His father searched for him in Madras and Tiruchirapalli. Little is known of how he was finally found but, by September, he was back with his family.

A year after his failure in Kumbakonam, Ramanujan decided to give college another try in Madras. In 1906,

Pachaiyappa's College was a respectable institution in Madras, open only to Hindus. Ramanujan arrived one day at Egmore Railway Station to join Pachaiyappa. Exhausted by the journey, he fell asleep in the waiting room of the station. A man woke him up, took him to his house, fed him and directed him to the college.

To succeed in the university examination was the ambition of every young man those days, as a degree was a sure passport to a good career. Ramanujan, eighteen years old now, aimed to be a degree holder. His new mathematics teacher, impressed by his notebooks, got the principal to give him a partial scholarship. When the master solved a problem in algebra or trigonometry using a dozen mathematical steps, Ramanujan would solve it in three or four steps. He would often work out the key steps in his head, leaving his classmates confused. Sometimes he worked with the college's senior maths professor, P Singaravelu Muthaliar, who was impressed by Ramanujan's brilliance. Together, the two of them went over problems that appeared in mathematical journals.

Life was  financially tough for Ramanujan. He found it difficult to make both ends meet. One day, the wind blew his cap off as he boarded the electric train. His Sanskrit teacher, who was particular that the boys covered their traditional tufts, asked him to buy a new one. Ramanujan apologised and said that he did not even have the few annas that it cost. His classmates pooled their money together and bought the cap for him.

Everyone was impressed by Ramanujan's intellectual gifts. Unfortunately, his experience at Kumbakonam repeated itself here. If English was the problem at Kumbakonam, it was physiology in Madras. He found the subject boring and repulsive. A strict vegetarian, he hated the idea of cutting up frogs. In an examination on the digestive system, he wrote a few lines in the answer sheet and handed it over unsigned. 'Sir, this is my undigested product of the Digestion chapter.' The professor had no difficulty in identifying whose paper it was.

Except for mathematics, he did poorly in all the subjects. While he could finish a three-hour mathematics exam in thirty minutes, he failed all other examinations for two consecutive years. The higher education system of south India at the start of the 20th century had no place for Ramanujan. Everyone knew that he was gifted, but that was not enough to get him a degree.

The system had no place for an eccentric genius like him. So without a degree or a job, he languished at home in Kumbakonam.

His father's income of Rs 20 per month was barely enough for the family. Ramanujan went hungry at times. Sometimes an old woman in the neighbourhood would feed him. The family of his friend, S M Subramanyam, also gave him meals from time to time. To earn some money, Ramanujan decided to tutor students. One student, for Rs 7 a month, was Viswanatha Sastri, son of a Government College philosophy professor. Everyday, Ramanujan walked to the boy's house on Solaiappa Mudaliar Street and taught him algebra, geometry and trigonometry. The trouble was that he taught one method on a particular day and, if the student forgot this method, he would teach a totally new method the next day. He also posed complicated questions, which the student found difficult to understand. He also wandered into areas schoolteachers rarely touched. For instance, if they discussed the height of a wall as part of a trigonometry problem, Ramanujan insisted that its height was only relative. 'Can you say how high it seems to an ant or a buffalo?' he would ask. The students were puzzled by these philosophical observations. Viswanatha Shastri found Ramanujan inspiring but the other students did not. So he proved to be a failure as a tutor in the subject he loved.

However, his academic failures enabled him to develop unconventionally. He was left undisturbed to pursue mathematics. He received no guidance, no stimulation, just the few rupees that he got from tutoring. His family and friends did not discourage him or demand that he find work.

To Ramanujan, mathematics was closely connected to his faith, his belief in the goddess Namagiri. Later, when he went to England, he would build a theory of reality around zero and infinity, though his friends were at a loss to know what he meant by it. Zero, according to him, represented Absolute Reality. Infinity was the myriad forms of that Reality. He found spiritual meaning in mathematics. For Ramanujan, numbers and their mathematical relationships showed how the universe fit together. He said, 'An equation for me has no meaning unless it expresses a thought of God.' Once when he was twenty-one, he visited the house of a teacher. In the course of a conversation, he spoke at length on the ties he saw between God, zero and infinity, keeping everyone spellbound till two in the morning.

# The Householder

At the age of twenty, Ramanujan had no degrees, had flunked out of two colleges, had no job and no interest in anything but mathematics. He was short and stocky; his clean-shaven face was pock-marked. His forehead was adorned with the red-and-white caste mark. The front of his head was shaved while the rest of his hair was pulled back and tied in a tuft. This made him look very fat. However, he walked with his head held high and with a sprightly gait. When he got excited, the words tumbled out of him.

He was usually found seated on the pial of his house on Sarangapani Sannidhi Street, madly scribbling on a large slate held on his lap. For a long time, his parents put up with him. Then, his mother decided to get him married in the hope that that would make him more responsible.

In 1908, when Ramanujan's mother was visiting friends in the village of Rajendram, about 60 miles from Kumbakonam, she saw a young girl called Janaki. She was the daughter of a distant relative. Horoscopes were matched and discussions began. Janaki's family had seen better times. Her father dealt in jewellery making and had once owned some property. Now, having fallen on hard times, he could not offer much dowry. Ramanujan was not considered an attractive son-in-law. To Komalathammal, this seemed to be an ideal match for her son. His father, however, protested. Their son could do better than that, he argued. However, Komalathammal's word was law and no one paid any heed to her husband's protests. Ramanujan's father stayed at home and did not accompany them for the wedding the following July.

Janaki's sister, Vijayalakshmi, was also to be married on the same day. The other bridegroom showed up on time, but there was no sign of Ramanujan and family till late at night. Janaki's father threatened to marry her off to someone else—probably his nephew. The train from Kumbakonam rolled hours late into the station nearest to Rajendram. By the time they reached the venue of the marriage in a bullock cart from the station, it was past midnight. Janaki's father, his patience stretched to breaking point, wanted to call off the wedding. But Komalathammal's persuasive powers won the day.

And so Ramanujan married Janaki, then nine years old. Janaki was simple and pretty. She was to join her husband only after three years. So outwardly nothing changed in his life after marriage. At heart, however, Ramanujan knew that he was no longer a free spirit. He had a wife, his father was getting old; it was high time that he assumed the duties of an adult. And he badly needed a job, to plan his future, to plan a new life. Again, he set out for Madras.

At Madras, he stayed at the Victoria Students Hostel with Viswanatha Sastri whom he had tutored. Each morning Ramanujan would set out in search of students to tutor. He did not succeed because, unfortunately, the news of his complicated ways of teaching had preceded him. Ramanujan was upset. Viswanatha Sastri consoled him saying that his talent would be recognised in due course. Ramanujan replied sadly that a great man like Galileo had died misunderstood and under house arrest. It would be his turn too to die in poverty.

The only assets he had with him were two large notebooks stuffed with mathematics. In a society where wealth mattered and academic degrees commanded respect, Ramanujan had only his notebooks to vouch for his knowledge. However, people liked his friendly and gregarious nature. To his friends, he was full of fun, always punning on Tamil and English words, telling jokes and stories. He could talk on any subject, his eyes mischievous and sparkling.

He was a simple man, with simple needs and manners. He was intelligent, persistent and hard working, but nobody could help him acquire a job. With recommendation letters from professors and other senior people, he went knocking on doors. He met V Ramaswami who had founded the Indian Mathematical Society. Ramaswami recommended that he meet P V Seshu Iyer, a charter member of the Mathematical Society. However, nothing came of it.

In December 1910, Ramanujan went to see R Ramachandra Rao, who was the District Collector of Nellore. His contemporary and friend, C V Rajagopalachari, assured Ramachandra Rao of Ramanujan's ability. Though he could not give Ramanujan a job, he promised to pay him an allowance of Rs 25. It was not much, but it freed him from economic worries. Ramanujan was happy. He was surrounded by friends and felt carefree and cheerful. He often stayed up late into the night, exclaiming about astronomical wonders,. A friend, whose sleep was disturbed by Ramanujan's monologue, poured a pot of water over him, apparently to cool his head. Ramanujan did not mind. He took everything in his stride.

In 1911, Ramanujan's first paper appeared in the *Journal of the Indian Mathematical Society*. This propelled him into the limelight both at home and abroad. Ramanujan was mathematically productive at this time. He published interesting problems in the Mathematical Society journal, one after another. However, he was unemployed and did not have enough money to buy paper. He needed four reams of paper a month. For want of paper, he sometimes wrote in red ink on paper already written upon.

Ramanujan got a temporary job at the Madras Accountant General's office for Rs 20 per month, but he lasted there only a few weeks. So again, with the help of Ramachandra Rao, he applied for a job at the Madras

Port Trust. On 1 March 1912, three weeks after he applied for the job, he was appointed as a clerk in the accounts section, earning Rs 30 per month and working under Sir Francis Spring and S Narayana Iyer. Now that he had a steady income, his wife Janaki, along with Ramanujan's mother, came to stay with him. They all stayed with his grandmother in a little house on Saiva Muthiah Mudali Street, off Broadway, George Town. It was a tiny house, for which they paid Rs 3 per month as rent.

Ramanujan worked on mathematics before he left for the office in the morning and again after he came home. Sometimes he sat up till six the next morning, grabbing two or three hours of sleep before rushing to work. Even in the office, after completing his allotted work, he indulged in mathematics. Luckily, his bosses did not mind his interest in mathematics.

Narayana Iyer, a member of the Mathematical Society, had a fondness for Ramanujan. In the evenings, both would go to the elder man's house on Pycrofts Road in Triplicane. There, sitting on the porch, they did mathematical problems on their slates till midnight. Narayana Iyer was a good mathematician. Nevertheless, Ramanujan's habit of collapsing many steps into one left him dazed. Many times he said, 'Descend to my level of understanding and write at least ten steps between the two steps of yours.' 'Why? Wasn't it obvious?' would be Ramanujan's answer. Finally, after a lot of cajoling, he would agree to expand his solution to the problem.

Narayana Iyer convinced Sir Francis Spring that Ramanujan was indeed a rough diamond, a genius, a remarkable mathematician. The Britisher too realised that he was someone special, but how special and gifted, they were not sure. Everyone agreed that he was a man with a taste for mathematics and tremendous ability. Yet no help was forthcoming. His friends and well-wishers advised him to write to Cambridge or elsewhere in the West for help since no one in India understood him. So Ramanujan wrote to H F Baker, a great mathematician, seeking help or advice but was politely turned down. He next wrote to E W Hobson, an equally distinguished mathematician, but he too said, 'No.'

On 16 January 1913, Ramanujan wrote to another Cambridge mathematician, G H Hardy, who at thirty-five, was already well known as a brilliant mathematician. The letter began as follows:

*Dear Sir,*

*I beg to introduce myself to you as a clerk in the Accounts Department of the Port Trust Office at Madras on a salary of only 20 pounds per annum. I am now about 23 years of age. I have had no University education but I have undergone the ordinary school course. After leaving school I have been employing the spare time at my disposal to work at Mathematics. I have not trodden through the conventional regular course which is followed in a University course, but I am striking out a new path for myself. I have made a special investigation of divergent series in general and the results I get are termed by the local mathematicians as "startling".*

The concluding paragraph read:

*I would request you to go through the enclosed papers. Being poor, if you are convinced that there is anything of value I would like to have my theorems published. I have not given the actual investigations nor the expressions that I get but I have indicated the lines on which I proceed. Being inexperienced I would very highly value any advice you give me. Requesting to be excused for the trouble I give you.*

*I remain,*

*Dear Sir,*

*Yours truly,*

*S Ramanujan.*

# The Dawn of Fame

Ramanujan's name will always be linked with that of Godfrey Harold Hardy. It was Hardy's understanding of his genius that brought about a complete turning point in Ramanujan's career. His letter to Hardy ran into eleven pages. Written in large, legible, rounded schoolboy script, it was filled with theorems in the divergent series. When Hardy first read the letter, his reaction was that Ramanujan was just an Indian crank. So he put the manuscripts aside and immersed himself in his daily tasks. In the evening, he went through Ramanujan's theorems again and was intrigued. Hardy was perhaps the finest of England's mathematicians, with the best education and in touch with the latest mathematical thought. Yet Ramanujan's theorems left him bewildered. Like the Indian mathematicians, Hardy did not know what to make of his work. He doubted his own judgement of it. So he consulted his colleague, another great mathematician, John Edensor Littlewood. Both probed the theorems before them and decided that there was much more in Ramanujan's formulae than met the eye. The more they studied the theorems, the more dazzled they became. Hardy would rank Ramanujan's letter as 'certainly the most remarkable I have ever received…its author, a mathematician of the highest quality, a man of altogether exceptional originality and power.'

Hardy's reply was full of appreciation and encouragement, but he particularly demanded to see proofs of the theorems. Hardy wrote, 'I want particularly to see your proofs of your assertions here. You will understand that, in this theory, everything depends on rigorous exactitude of proof.'

Hardy felt it would be best if Ramanujan came to Cambridge. However, religious beliefs forbade Brahmins from crossing the seas. In those days, a Brahmin travelling to Europe or America was accused of going against his faith. The result was exclusion from caste. And if you lost caste, it meant that friends and relatives would exclude you from all rituals and functions. You would not be allowed into temples or get any help for the funeral of a family member. Ramanujan was from a very orthodox Brahmin family and so he was not willing to go to Cambridge.

In the meantime, Hardy's recommendation had its effect in Madras too. The officials were ready to bend the rules for him, even though he did not have a degree. By 12 April, Ramanujan was awarded a scholarship, which set him free to pursue mathematics, to attend lectures at the university and to use its library. He and his family now lived in a little house in Hanumantharayan Koil Street in Triplicane. With a research scholarship in hand and on leave from Port Trust, Ramanujan had nothing to do but pursue his passion. And he threw himself into mathematics, leaving day-to-day cares to others. In Janaki's words, he would ask his mother or grandmother to wake him up at midnight, so that he could go on working in the silent cool hours of the night. Sometimes, he had to be reminded to eat. At other times, they would serve him curd rice or sambar rice in his study so that his train of thought would not be broken. According to Janaki, whenever she opened her eyes, she saw him working. The scratching of the stylus on the slate sounded through the house the whole day and night.

Ramanujan, the special research student, was a hot topic in Madras. Everyone wondered how he had attained such an intellectual position without the help of books or teachers.

Hardy sent three letters to Ramanujan asking for rigorous proofs for his theorems. Ramanujan, however, held back, offering excuses. Finally, Hardy requested Eric Harold Neville, his colleague and friend who was visiting Madras for lectures, to somehow persuade Ramanujan to visit Cambridge. Neville and Ramanujan struck a bond instantly and just after three meetings Ramanujan asked Neville whether he would like to take the notebooks to study at leisure. Neville considered this a great compliment as the priceless notebooks had never been out of Ramanujan's hands. Neville had won his trust. Neville took the opportunity to ask him whether he would come to Cambridge and, to his delight and surprise, Ramanujan agreed at once.

What miracle had brought about the sudden change? It is said that some friends and well-wishers of Ramanujan had been able to convince his mother— the key obstacle to his going—to agree to the trip. But Ramanujan, religious as always, believed that his mother had a dream in which she was surrounded by Europeans and heard the Goddess Namagiri commanding her to allow her son to fulfil his life's purpose. In late December of 1913, K Narayana Iyer, a family friend, Ramanujan and his mother set out to Namakkal to visit the Namagiri temple. For three nights, they slept in the temple grounds. On the third night, Ramanujan rose from a dream and woke Narayana Iyer. He said that a flash of brilliant light had appeared before him and asked him to bypass the injunction against foreign travel. It is possible that Ramanujan's wish to go to England warred with his strong devotion to Namagiri and so he found a socially acceptable way to go without offending his family's wishes. Ramanujan always said that he had been divinely inspired to go to Cambridge.

Once the decision was made, Neville set all his other fears to rest. First of all, his travel and living expenses would be taken care of. His English was good enough for him to manage at Cambridge. His preference for vegetarian food would be respected. Ramanujan could not bear the thought of writing any examinations. Neville assured him that he would not have to write any.

All was not well, however, on the family front. His father-in-law wondered why he could not pursue mathematics in India. Ramanujan was not always in the best of health. His mother worried that his indifferent health might suffer in the English cold. To remain a vegetarian without Indian food would be difficult. The locals might view him with prejudice. Many of his friends saw it as an attempt to transfer to the English university the glory and fame that belonged to Madras. Neville, however, convinced them all that the trip was in Ramanujan's own interest. It would only help him reach the zenith of glory. And so by Neville's and Hardy's sincere efforts, a scholarship was approved for Ramanujan and he got ready to leave for England.

His friends coached him in western ways. His 'kutumi' had to go. He had to wear western clothes. He was taught to use a fork and knife. However, all this did not excite Ramanujan. He was worried about how he would stay vegetarian in England. He hated his western haircut. He felt uncomfortable with the clothes he had to wear. The day before he was to leave, he walked into the faculty room of the Presidency College with a big suitcase, which he opened to display the western clothes bought for him.

How was he to wear them? Tying the knot on his tie puzzled him. He tried to joke about it, but his friends knew that he was unhappy. He would miss the streets filled with bullock carts, their bells jingling from painted horns, bare-chested men in dhotis, women in saris, their nose rings and bangles shining against their dark skin, the sweet smell of jasmine flowers and the pungent smell of burning cow dung. What was in store for him in England? His friends stayed with him all night, trying to calm his frayed nerves.

On the morning of his departure, an official send-off was held in his honour, organised by Srinivasa Iyengar, the advocate general. Narayana Iyer had a strange request at that time. He asked whether he could exchange slates with Ramanujan. He hoped that he would gain inspiration from the slate during Ramanujan's absence.

Ramanujan was in tears. He had dispatched his family to Kumbakonam. His life had taken a sudden turn. He had been an unknown boy sitting alone on the pial of his house in Kumbakonam. Now the elite of Madras had turned out to see him off. He was a drop-out from the Government College. Now he was bound for Trinity College, Cambridge. He had struggled to obtain three rupees to go to Madras from his village. Now he was taking a four-hundred-rupee fare journey to England.

His present position was the fruit of his hard work and a little luck. However, he still feared of the unknown. His friends knew that he was unhappy. He was going as if obeying a call.

The British India Lines Ship *S S Nevasa* was to take him to England. Ramanujan was introduced to the captain and the passengers. Among them was Dr Muthu, a tuberculosis specialist. There was good cheer and light banter. But Ramanujan was in tears according to his friends.

At about 10 am on 17 March 1914, the *Nevasa* slipped slowly away from the dock, with Ramanujan on board. Over the days, he began to enjoy the voyage. He mingled with the passengers and ate vegetarian food. He sent letters to friends in India and, on 14 April, the *Nevasa* arrived at the mouth of the Thames.

# At Home in Cambridge

Neville and his older brother came to London to meet Ramanujan. Neville took Ramanujan to Cromwell Road where the National India Association had offices, in the hope that it would make him feel more at home. It did not. It was a strange new world for him. In population, London was ten times larger than Madras. In the streets of London, he heard the nasal cockney slang; he found every sort of Englishman in bowler hats and flat working men's caps, women in finery and in rags.

Ramanujan survived the initial shock and followed Neville to Cambridge. He stayed in Neville's house on Chesterton Road, in a little suburb of Cambridge. The house was spacious and Ramanujan had a measure of privacy. Hardy and Neville took care of the fees and paperwork needed to get his name in the first-year students' list. It was spring, with lovely, warm weather and flowers blooming everywhere. Ramanujan started to work with Hardy and Littlewood. He worked hard and was happy and productive. He attended a few lectures. Some were Hardy's and others were by Arthur Berry, a King's College mathematician in his early fifties.

One day, while working out a formula on the blackboard, Berry glanced around and noticed Ramanujan's face, glowing with excitement. Berry asked if he wanted to contribute something. Ramanujan went to the blackboard and wrote down the results that Berry had not yet proved.

Soon word got around about him. People did not often see him because he was always busy in his rooms. However, Neville's house was a far walk from Hardy's rooms. In early June, Ramanujan moved into rooms closer to where Hardy stayed. He was sad to leave Neville, because the two had developed a mutual trust and liking for each other. But Ramanujan had much to learn in mathematics and needed to be in an atmosphere of discussion and debate.

Ramanujan's notebooks contained thousands of theorems, corollaries and examples. Page after page they stretched on, with no proof or explanations. It exasperated the many mathematicians who tried to analyse them. Figuring out a single pair of modular equations took almost a month. They compared him to Leonhard Euler, a Swiss mathematician and Carl Jacobi, a Prussian mathematician, two towering figures on the stage of mathematical history in the 18th century. Hardy, studying Ramanujan's notebooks, saw that they were worth publishing. And so his notebook entries began to take on a new form as mathematical papers fit to be seen and read by the world. In south India, though Ramanujan had Narayana Iyer and Seshu Iyer who were in awe of his brain, no one had been able to truly appreciate his work. He had been alone. He had had no peers. Now in Littlewood and Hardy he had them. The fact that he had, in Cambridge, a community of mathematicians who understood his work more than made up for his being a stranger in an alien land.

Ramanujan found western accessories cumbersome. He felt as if the metal knives and forks pierced his mouth. He grumbled that shoes pinched his feet. He found the coat, trousers and tie suffocating. The vegetables were tastless. All Englishmen looked alike to him. But despite all these petty miseries, he was a happy man. He found his mathematical experiments exciting. He was not short of money and could devote every waking moment to mathematics. Ramanujan was in a state of ecstasy.

Ramanujan sometimes said that the answers to complex mathematical problems came to his mind through the blessings of the goddess Namagiri. Westerners called it intuition. Here was a man who could work out modular equations and complicated theorems and had a mastery over fractions. But all his results new or old, right or wrong, were got by intuition and induction, for which he could not give any logical explanation. He was sometimes wrong, and he lacked the mathematical knowledge to tell when he was right and when he was wrong. He stated correct and incorrect theorems with the same innocent confidence. He had no clear-cut idea of what was meant by proof. It was Ramanujan's good fortune that he got to work with Hardy, the apostle of proof.

Hardy set to work on him, to get rid of this flaw—the price Ramanujan had to pay for his isolation in his early years. Ramanujan gradually absorbed new points of view and his later papers read like the works of a well-informed mathematician.

# Hard Times at Cambridge

Then World War I began. Europe marched to war with flags flying. Everyone, including the troops, expected it to be over in a month or two. Unexpectedly, it turned out to be a terrible war, going on for year after year.

Cambridge too felt the impact of the war. Littlewood was called to serve as a second lieutenant in the Royal Garrison Artillery. With Littlewood away, Ramanujan was more dependent on Hardy than ever. The war had its unpleasant effects on Ramanujan too. Peaceful Cambridge had been transformed into a training camp and hospital. Food prices rose by a third. Intellectual communication with German mathematicians was cut off.

Ramanujan wrote home regularly, assuring his family that he was observing his vegetarianism and religious practices. His letters to his friends spoke of his work and progress. He sent parcels of English literature books to his two brothers in India. Ramanujan's letters to his father reminded him about the maintenance of his house, but his letters to his mother spoke about the great war and the problems unleashed by it. He mentioned the exact number of men fighting, the width of the battlefronts, the use of aeroplanes in combat and the participation and support of the Indian rajas toward the war. He knew that such an account would interest her.

But Ramanujan was ill at ease. The bother of finding and preparing food for himself affected his well-being. The icy chill of the English winter, the tight clothes he had to wear, the absence of letters from Janaki—all troubled him. One cold night in Cambridge, his Bengali friend, P C Mahalanobis, saw Ramanujan huddled by the fire in his room. 'Are you warm at night?' he asked Ramanujan. 'No,' replied Ramanujan. It came to light that Ramanujan, unable to bear the cold, slept with his overcoat on and a shawl wrapped around him. 'Maybe he doesn't have enough blankets,' thought Mahalanobis and looked at his bed on the other side of the fireplace. The bedspread was loose, but the blankets lay absolutely intact, tucked neatly under the mattress. Ramanujan had enough blankets. But he had not known what to do with them. Gently and patiently, his friend showed him the way to turn back the blankets, slip into the bed and pull the warm covers over him.

In spite of these discomforts, Ramanujan was happy with his work. Doing mathematics satisfied the deep emotional and intellectual needs in him. And like any other human being, he longed for recognition. In 1915, nine of his papers appeared—five of them in English journals and one in the *Journal of the Indian Mathematical Society*.

He was now a popular, even legendary, figure in Cambridge. He mixed freely with both English and Indians. Ramanujan's tutor, E W Barnes, called him the most brilliant of all the top Trinity students who had come to him. With his scholarship extended for one more year, Ramanujan was financially comfortable in England. He sent a little of the amount to his family in India. In March 1916, he received a BA, 'by research' on the basis of his long paper on highly composite numbers.

To all who knew him, it appeared that Ramanujan had adjusted well to a foreign country and alien life. But doing mathematics and adjusting to an alien culture drained him of all personal energy. It took a toll on his physical and emotional strength. Most of the academics relaxed in the evenings at the dining hall. The camaraderie eased the pressure of the day's hard work. Littlewood, Neville and Hardy enjoyed the fun, but not Ramanujan. Owing to his strict vegetarian principles, he cooked in the alcove, just off his sitting room, and ate alone. When he could get the ingredients, he cooked rice, sambar and rasam. He had fruits and curd otherwise.

Ramanujan was not one to embrace a foreign culture. He was a son of Kumbakonam, who had great respect for his parents' wishes. He remained steadfastly vegetarian and performed the Hindu rituals in front of the poster of a deity that he had put up in his room. For his daily puja, he wore a dhoti, applied namam to his forehead, performed the puja and then wiped it off. Only then did he wear his western clothes. Memories of his life back at home often haunted him. The aroma of his mother's cooking, the bright colours of the religious festivals, the reds and oranges of the women's clothes, the vibrant green of the vegetation, the smell of burning cow dung, the bright blue sky and the hot sun—he missed them all. The war and the winter made things worse. His only delight was working with Hardy.

Hardy, in fact, was the best and truest friend he had. He was loyal and kind, but was a stern taskmaster. Though friendly and encouraging, he insisted that work should not suffer. So if Ramanujan wanted to relax and even once in a way stay away from mathematics, Hardy never supported the idea. Even when Ramanujan was in hospital, Hardy hoped he would soon get well so that both of them could together solve some complex problems. Hardy's urgings often made Ramanujan feel guilty that he was sick and unable to do mathematics. By early 1917, after three years of Cambridge, his life was ruled by the four walls of his room, Hardy and mathematics. He would sometimes work for thirty hours at a stretch and then sleep for twenty hours. Regularity, balance and rest disappeared from his life. He was sacrificing his life at the altar of mathematics.

In Hardy he had intellectual companionship, but without his mother or Janaki to prepare his meals and serve him, with no one to remind him to sleep, no one to cool his fevered brow, to calm, to counsel and lead, Ramanujan felt alone. His mission was achieved, but he was more than a mind. His body had needs that his mind could not fulfil. In those days, Indians who came to study in England, facing an alien and hostile climate, risked their health, especially those from the South who were inclined to develop tuberculosis and disease of the chest.

Ramanujan had never attached any importance to food. In England, it became an awful bother. South Indian food was not easy to prepare and Ramanujan preferred to use his time to work on challenging problems. His strict vegetarianism also cost him his health, especially during wartime. Food was rationed. Prices rose. There was shortage of all foodstuffs. When potatoes and sugar were not available for the English, the vegetables and fruits that Ramanujan craved were naturally hard to come by. Ramanujan had started to feel the direct effects of war. Food shortages, irregular food habits, isolation, overwork and the climate left him open to disease. His lifestyle in his third year in England caused his illness.

# A Great Mind, A Troubled Soul

By spring 1917, Hardy wrote to the University of Madras that Ramanujan was afflicted with some incurable disease. He was suffering from malnutrition. It was an anxious time when he was admitted in hospital. However, soon he was better and out of hospital. Hardy himself nursed him for a while. But Ramanujan was a terrible patient, difficult to manage. He was fussy about food, did not obey the doctor, forever complained about his aches and pains and had no faith in medicines. He was finally admitted to the Mendip Hills Sanatorium at Hill Grove in Somerset. There he was treated by Dr Muthu, the tuberculosis specialist he had met on the *Nevasa*. Even in the sanatorium, Ramanujan wanted to do mathematics. He was unhappy because of the cold (open-air treatment for tuberculosis was the accepted norm in those days) and also because of his dislike for the food that was served at the sanatorium. Other reasons too contributed to his unhappiness. There was trouble back home—domestic tension. His possessive mother was trying to distance Janaki from him. They had frequent arguments with harsh words and hard feelings. His mother intercepted the letters Janaki wrote to him. Consequently, Janaki stopped writing to him and she left his home. All this distressed Ramanujan.

In 1916, Ramanujan's tutor, Barnes, had written to the University of Madras to say that  considering his achievements, it was a possibility that Ramanujan would be elected a Fellow of Trinity College. But by October 1917, nothing had come of it. As a result, Ramanujan felt gloomier.

Around that time, he shifted to Matlock, located about 150 miles north west of London. English sanatoriums were not likely to lift anyone's spirits. Ramanujan felt cold and miserable all the time. He was too sick to be productive in mathematics. This depressed him further. The doctors were not to his liking. He did not get the food he craved. What he ate, he did not relish. He longed for south Indian food and emotional support from his family.

Hardy's concern for Ramanujan's health moved him to press for recognition for his friend. But Ramanujan was still writhing under the humiliating blow he had suffered when Trinity had turned him down. He wrote to his family in India after remaining silent for about one year. Outwardly he seemed to have accepted the flow of events. So no one guessed that there was a storm brewing in his heart. Rejected by Trinity, seemingly abandoned by his wife, sick and helpless, unable to produce mathematical wonders others expected of him, he was overcome by shame. With Littlewood and Neville away, he had no one to confide in. His relationship with Hardy was different. He did not feel free enough to bare his soul to him. As a result, the tumultuous emotions raging in his heart boiled over, forcing him to take the extreme step of attempting suicide.

One day in January or February of 1918, at a London Underground station, Ramanujan threw himself onto the tracks in front of an approaching train. Luckily, a guard spotted him and pulled a switch, bringing the train to a screeching halt a few feet in front of him. He was arrested by the Scotland Yard, but Hardy somehow managed to get him released.

Late in February, Ramanujan was elected to the Cambridge Philosophical Society, which raised his spirits. About ten days later, he received a telegram from Hardy which said that he had been named a Fellow of the Royal Society. The whole of India was thrilled. His delighted friends wrote to him. Hearing about his ill-health and the food rationing, they sent him plenty of foodstuffs from India. However, his physical state was pathetic. He was frail, thin and emaciated.

It was as though he was killing himself by slow starvation. Diet is a very important part of tuberculosis cure. Scrambled eggs, tea, rice with chillies and mustard fried in butter and so on were served to him, but these were not to his taste. His friend A S Ramalingam tried to send him some foodstuffs that he liked. He offered to cook for Ramanujan. This, however, was not permitted by the authorities of the hospital. Ramanujan stubbornly stuck to his vegetarianism at the cost of his health. He even refused to eat porridge, oatmeal and cream. He wanted only south Indian food. Consequently, his condition worsened.

Ramanujan was now moved to a small hospital in the heart of London. Though he saw several specialists, the diagnosis was still uncertain. Sudden outbursts of high fever gripped him at intervals. He had a pain no one could trace. In the meantime, he was awarded the Trinity Fellowship in 1918, thanks to the efforts of Littlewood and Hardy. This cheered him.

Shortly after, the war ended. Hardy felt that a trip to India would do Ramanujan good. He wrote to Francis Dewsbury, registrar of the University of Madras, about it. It was safe to travel, Ramanujan's health had improved, he had gained about fifteen pounds and his temperature had steadied. The suggestion was to be made tactfully without hurting Ramanujan's sensitivities. So he was offered a job as university professor with a salary of about Rs 400 per month. The university also awarded him a fellowship of 250 pounds per year. This was over and above the amount awarded to him by Trinity. Ramanujan remembered his hard days in Kumbakonam when his scholarship had been withdrawn and his time in Madras when he had to depend on the patronage of Ramachandra Rao and the few rupees he got from tutoring. In a letter to

Dewsbury, while thanking him for the generous help, Ramanujan stated that the surplus money after his and his parents' expenses were met should be utilised to provide school fees for poor boys and orphans and for books in schools.

# The Homecoming

On March 13, 1919, Ramanujan set sail for India. When he stepped off the ship at Bombay, his mother and brother were there to meet him, but not Janaki. Domestic conflict had ruined his spirits for the last three years in England. Now it put a damper on the joy of his arrival in India. Ignoring his mother's protests, he sent for Janaki.

Komalathammal had planned to take Ramanujan to Rameswaram for a purification ceremony, to wash away the taint caused by his overseas trip. But his sickly appearance made her decide against it. After a few nights in Bombay, they left for Madras.

Everyone in India knew Ramanujan by now. The story of his humble origins, his brilliant career and his elevation to the Royal Society had been in the news. On his arrival, he was offered the university professorship, which he said he would accept when his health improved. The cream of Madras society visited him. To them he was a hero, someone who had shown the West the genius of south India. They all wanted to bear his expenses, medical and otherwise, and numerous homes wanted to host him. He shifted to a place called Venkata Vilas on Luz Church Road. Janaki and her brother joined him there. She was eighteen now. A closeness developed between them that had never been there before.

Everyone knew that Ramanujan was a changed man physically. It was the change in his personality that surprised and disturbed his friends. Once cheerful and affectionate, he was now depressed, sullen and cold. His illness had made him bitter, short-tempered and peevish. He snapped at the slightest provocation. Even his faith seemed to have been affected. When someone spoke about temples, he retorted, '… they were only devils.' The quarrels between Komalathammal and Janaki upset him. The doctors advised him to move inland to escape the Madras summer. His mother opted for Kodumudi, a small town near his birthplace.

Around this time, Ramanujan openly rebelled against his mother's possessiveness. He craved Janaki's companionship, but his jealous mother wanted to send her away. Ramanujan respectfully, but firmly, put his foot down and insisted that Janaki stay with him. Janaki took care of him, gave his medicines and nursed him all night. Ramanujan would say to her, 'If only you had come with me to England, perhaps I would not have fallen ill.'

After two months at Kodumudi, they moved to Kumbakonam. Despite the best medical help, little could be done for his health for the simple reason that Ramanujan seemed to have lost the will to live. His doctor, P S Chandrasekhara Iyer, wanted him to return to Madras where the climate and surroundings were more suited to an invalid. But Ramanujan, tired out by two years of medical opinions and treatments, resisted the move. Finally, in January 1920, he was persuaded to return to Madras.

The only silver lining in this morbid state of affairs was his mathematics. His intellectual vision grew keener and brighter as though approaching death was inspiring a flurry of creativity. He wrote in detail to Hardy about mock-theta functions. He expressed interest in subscribing to new mathematical journals. Ramanujan's discovery on mock-theta functions testified that his skill and originality had not been affected by his approaching death. He filled page after page with theorems and computational fragments. When the American mathematician, George Andrews, browsed through them half a century later, he was spellbound by its richness and surprises and wondered how someone could think up such wonders. During his last months, his relationship with Janaki was relaxed and warm. According to her, he was kind to her, his conversation was full of wit and humour and he was always cracking jokes to cheer her up. He narrated tales of England and of his visits to various places of interest there. He knew he was dying and tried to put up a cheerful front.

But in general, he was sullen and angry, raving at one thing or the other. He was  skin and bones and complained of pain. Nevertheless, through all this pain and fever, his head propped against the pillows, he sat up and worked on his mathematics. Janaki dutifully collected all the papers and kept them safe in a big leather box. In her words, it was 'always mathematics. Even four days before his death, he was scribbling.' Early on 20 April 1920, he became unconscious. Around mid-morning he breathed his last. His wife, parents, brothers and friends were with him. He was just thirty-two years old.

Most of his orthodox Brahmin relatives stayed away from his funeral. As Ramanujan had not undergone the purification ceremony after his overseas trip, they considered him impure. Ramachandra Rao arranged the cremation, with the help of his son-in-law and Ramanujan's friend, Rajagopalachari.

# A Lasting Legacy

Though Ramanujan died young, the work he did in his short life earned him his place in history. His intuitive discoveries puzzle mathematicians even decades after his death. His papers are still probed for more secrets.

Today Ramanujan's work has applications in particle physics or in the calculation of pi up to a very large number of decimal places. His work on Rieman's Zeta Function has been applied to pyrometry, the investigations of the temperature of furnaces. His work on Partition Numbers has resulted in two applications—new fuels and fabrics such as nylons. His theorems are being applied in areas such as polymer chemistry, computers and recently cancer research. His work on mock-theta functions and modular equations are being studied for possible application to atomic research.

Crystallographer S Ramaseshan has proved how Ramanujan's work on partitions sheds light on plastics. Plastics are polymers, repeating molecular units that combine in various ways. His work on partitions—how smaller numbers combine to form larger ones—refers to this process. Computers, not even heard of in 1920, have also drawn from Ramanujan's work. The rise of computer algebra is one example. A modular equation in Ramanujan's notebooks led to computer algorithms for evaluating pi that are in use today. George Andrews once said with regard to Ramanujan, 'The rise of computer algebra makes it interesting to study someone who seems like he had a computer algebra package in his head.'

Ramanujan's life played a significant role in developing relations between India and England. Ramanujan was the first Indian whom the British acknowledged as equal to their greatest men. The notion that white is superior to black was successfully disproved by Ramanujan.

In 1921, Hardy published the last of Ramanujan's papers. In 1927, Cambridge University Press came out with Ramanujan's *Collected Papers*, 355 pages of everything he had ever published. Then followed a series of papers with titles such as 'Two Assertions Made by Ramanujan,' 'Note on a Problem of Ramanujan,' and 'Note on Ramanujan's Arithmetical Function r (n)'. A 1940 listing noted 105 papers devoted to his work since his death.

In 1950, a fantastic thing happened. S Ramaseshan, whose father had known Ramanujan, dropped in on some friends in Bombay. They took him to their printing plant where, in an inner room, he was, in the words of his biographer Robert Kanigel, 'shown a stack of browned old paper with magic squares and mathematical formulae written in elegant handwriting.' It was Ramanujan's famous 'frayed notebook.'

In 1957, The Tata Institute of Fundamental Research brought out Ramanujan's notebooks in two huge volumes. Ramaseshan's friends at the Commercial Printing Press were given the exciting task of publishing the 'frayed notebook' that had been found, so miraculously, on their premises.

Ramanujan's seventy-fifth birth anniversary was observed across south India. Town High School in

Kumbakonam named one of its building after him. A stamp was issued in his honour. The Indian postal service pointed out the potential applications of his work.

Hardy was once asked about his greatest contribution to mathematics and his reply was, 'the discovery of Ramanujan.' Some suggested that Ramanujan was 'Svayambu'—'self-born'. Kanigel described him as self-willed, self-directed, self-made.

India's first prime minister, Pandit Jawaharlal Nehru, said, 'Ramanujan's brief life and death are symbolic of conditions in India. Of our millions, how few get any education at all; how many live on the verge of starvation.'

Even now in India, youngsters cannot hope to get a reasonably good job unless they have a degree to boast of. Many times, Ramanujan came close to dying in obscurity, his potential not fully realised. His life is a lesson on the stumbling blocks he faced and how he overcame them successfully.

Robert Kanigel wrote, 'Ramanujan represented India's intellectual and spiritual strengths—but also its untapped potential.' If Ramanujan, with all the obstacles he had to encounter, could make the whole world sit up and notice him, there is hope for the gifted. Let us end our story on this optimistic note.

---

9 788183 687584